ROME

Christine Dugan, M.A.Ed.

PUBLISHING CREDITS

Content Consultant
Blane Conklin, Ph.D.

Associate Editor
Christina Hill, M.A.

Assistant Editor
Torrey Maloof

Editorial Assistants
Deborah Buchanan
Kathryn R. Kiley
Judy Tan

Editorial Director
Emily R. Smith, M.A.Ed.

Editor-in-Chief
Sharon Coan, M.S.Ed.

Editorial Manager
Gisela Lee, M.A.

Creative Director
Lee Aucoin

Cover Designer
Lesley Palmer

Designers
Deb Brown
Zac Calbert
Amy Couch
Robin Erickson
Neri Garcia

Publisher
Rachelle Cracchiolo, M.S.Ed.

Teacher Created Materials
5301 Oceanus Drive
Huntington Beach, CA 92649-1030
http://www.tcmpub.com
ISBN 978-0-7439-0432-2
© 2007 Teacher Created Materials, Inc.

TABLE OF CONTENTS

THE BEGINNING OF AN EMPIRE

According to legend, Rome was founded around 753 B.C. There were two brothers named Romulus (RAWM-yuh-luhs) and Remus (REE-muhs). The legends say they were raised by a wolf. One day, Romulus and Remus came upon an area of land. They decided to each build parts of a city. They fought over the sizes of their territories. Romulus killed Remus. Romulus became king of the city. He named the city Rome.

Kings ruled early Rome. Then, Rome became a **republic**. This meant that rulers were elected. The Roman Republic began in 509 B.C. and lasted almost 500 years.

Romulus ▶
and Remus
with their
wolf mother.

The Roman Republic had problems, though. The leaders in the Senate often argued about laws. They could not agree on public affairs. Also, many of Rome's citizens had no power in the republic. These common people were called **plebeians** (plih-BEE-uhnz). They revolted because they wanted to force the Senate to make changes.

▼ Roman senators debated important issues.

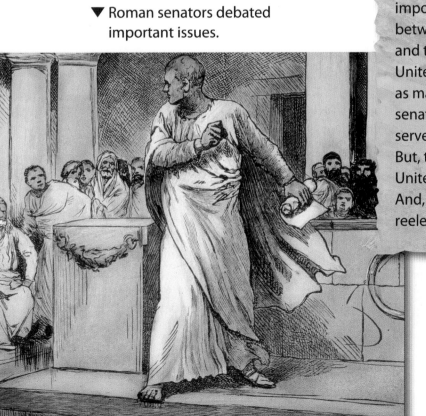

The Senate Then and Now

The United States government is a republic. And, it has a Senate. However, there are important differences between Rome's Senate and the Senate in the United States. There were as many as 600 Roman senators at one time. They served for their entire lives. But, there are only 100 United States senators. And, they must be reelected every six years.

THE RISE AND FALL OF JULIUS CAESAR

Julius Caesar (SEE-zuhr) was an important figure in the Roman Republic. Caesar was a powerful army general. He was well liked by his troops. Then, he made himself **dictator** after winning an important battle. This may have been a mistake for him.

Many Romans felt that Caesar was acting too much like a king. They did not want to go back to having kings in Rome. Some senators felt that Caesar was a threat to them. In 44 B.C., Caesar was stabbed to death by a group of senators.

Caesar's **heir** (AIR) was his adopted son, Gaius Octavius (GAY-uhs awk-TAY-vee-uhs). He was called Octavian. Octavian ruled Rome with two men named Mark Antony and Marcus Lepidus (LEP-uh-duhs).

▲ Roman senators stabbing Julius Caesar

These three men ruled together for seven years. Eventually, Octavian ruled alone.

In 27 B.C., the Senate changed Octavian's name to Augustus (oh-GUHS-tuhs). *Augustus* means "great." And, he became Rome's first emperor. This was the beginning of the Roman Empire. The Roman people loved him.

Caesar's Influence Continues

Caesar was an important person to the Romans. His name became a title for all Roman emperors. His name lived on in other ways, too. The Russian word *czar* (ZAWR) and the German word *kaiser* (KI-zuhr) are examples of this. Both of these words are based on Caesar's name.

What Month Is It?

Caesar introduced the 12-month calendar that is used today. Most of the month names are taken from Latin words. This includes *July*, which was named after Julius himself.

◀ The Julian Calendar was introduced in 46 B.C.

A Strong and Powerful Army

Many historians believe the Roman Empire was so strong because of the **legionnaires** (lee-juh-NEARZ). These were Rome's foot soldiers. They went into new lands. There, they fought to keep Rome in control.

Each legion had about 5,000 foot soldiers. Soldiers usually volunteered to join the army. An army legion did not just include soldiers. Doctors, cooks, and builders also traveled with the army.

▼ Roman roads still stand today.

The legionnaires were strong and brave. They fought in battles often. The army kept its men well armed. Soldiers used early weapons such as swords and daggers. They also wore heavy armor and helmets. This protected them from injuries.

◄ Roman soldiers

Roman Roads

Soldiers had to move quickly from one place to another. So, the army needed good roads to travel on. Romans tried to build roads as straight as possible. They ended up with an impressive system of paved roads. Many of these roads are still used today.

Strength in Numbers

The Roman army may have been the most successful army ever. Today, most countries try to keep their militaries strong.

BUILDING A CITY

The Romans were excellent builders. They copied some styles of architecture from ancient Greece. For example, they used arches and columns in bridges and buildings. But Romans had new ideas for buildings, too. They were the first people to use domes on buildings. Much of what they built is still standing today.

You may be surprised to learn that ancient Rome had a great water system. Their plumbing system helped send fresh water to houses and

The Pantheon ▼ in Rome has a huge dome.

▼ This is a Roman aqueduct in France.

Aqueducts

The Romans were the first to build **aqueducts** (AK-wuh-duhkts). These are pipes or channels that carry water from place to place. They are built above or below ground. Aqueducts helped the ancient cities get enough water. Visitors today can still see the incredible aqueducts.

Building Materials

Ancient Romans were the first to use concrete. This is a mixture of sand, gravel, cement, and water. This material is still used in most modern buildings and roads.

bathhouses. Many other cities based their water systems on what Rome had built.

Water was quite important to Romans. Rome can be a very hot place in the summer. Fresh water helped keep people cool. Romans built towns near rivers or springs so they could have a constant supply of fresh water.

City and Rural Life

Rome was a grand city. Visitors saw beautiful statues and buildings there. The Roman Forum was very impressive. However, not all of Rome was grand.

The city was also very noisy, dirty, and dangerous. Many Romans lived in close quarters. The buildings were run down. They often collapsed. Fires were common because people burned logs for cooking and heat.

Many Romans wanted to avoid the city. So, they lived in the country. The wealthiest Romans owned country **villas** (VIL-luhz).

▼ The Roman Forum was often crowded.

▲ Trajan's Market

Farms in the country produced everything a person needed. This included fruits and vegetables, milk, cheese, wine, and meat. Farmers relied on **slaves** to help with the crops.

◀ Mt. Vesuvius above the ruins of Pompeii

An Early Shopping Mall

Roman markets sold many kinds of goods. On the main streets were shops for shoes, pottery, food, and other important items. One such market was Trajan's (TRAY-juhnz) Market. This was named after Emperor Trajan.

The Clues at Pompeii

Pompeii was a town south of Rome. A volcano named Mt. Vesuvius (vuh-SUE-vee-uhs) was nearby. One day, it exploded and buried Pompeii. Remains of the town were dug up in the 1700s. We know a lot about the Roman Empire from clues found at Pompeii.

SOCIAL RANKINGS

Romans were not all considered equal within society. They were divided into three social classes. These classes were **citizens**, noncitizens, and slaves. Citizens had privileges that noncitizens did not. Owning property and voting are two examples.

▼ Slaves waited on wealthy men and women.

Slaves, both men and women, had no rights at all. Many slaves were born into slavery. Life conditions for the slaves varied. Some slaves were treated well by their masters. Others had to work long hours at hard jobs.

In a Roman family, the man was the ruler of the home. Men often spent a lot of time working away from their homes. This was especially true for men in the army. But they were still the most important members of their families.

Women were respected but had few rights. Women spent much of their time caring for their homes. They were not allowed to be citizens. That meant they could not be part of the Roman government.

◀ This toga shows that this man was powerful.

Money and Wealth

Social rank in ancient Rome was tied to money and wealth. This is still true in many cultures today. People are often divided into classes based on how much money they have. Today, though, people have more opportunities to move out of the lower classes.

Dress

A Roman man's clothes gave clues about his social class. All Romans wore **togas**. But, important men, like senators, wore togas with colored trim to show their power. Sometimes, the whole toga would be made out of a valuable material. Clothing was as important then as it is today.

EDUCATION FOR ROMAN CHILDREN

Children who lived in Rome did not all receive the same education. For example, students from the richest families had private tutors. Meanwhile, students from the poorest families did not go to school at all. They had to work from an early age.

Children from middle-class families started school at age 7. They went to school until the age of 12. Some girls also attended school. All students learned subjects like reading, writing, and math.

Things changed as children got older. Around the age of 12, students went on to attend what the Romans called grammar school. They read great works of literature. They also studied important writings. Girls rarely went to grammar school. They often stayed home to learn household skills from their mothers.

Around the age of 17, students could attend a rhetorical (rih-TORE-ih-kuhl) school. This was similar to what we call college today. Mostly rich boys attended these schools. They prepared for careers in law or government.

Many clocks ▶ use Roman numerals.

This is a stylus ▲ and part of a wax tablet.

Playtime

Marbles was a game played in Roman times. It is still played by children around the world today.

How Much is XXXVI?

Have you ever seen a watch, clock, or other object that uses symbols such as an X, V, or I? Maybe you have noticed this each year when it is Super Bowl time? These symbols are Roman numerals. Early Romans used them to represent their numbers. They are still used today.

Ancient Pens

Students did not have pens. Instead, each child wrote with a **stylus** (STI-luhs). This tool had a pointed end and a flat end. Students wrote letters or numbers with the pointed end, and the flat end was used to rub out mistakes. Students wrote on wax tablets.

LEISURE ACTIVITIES AND GAMES

Romans enjoyed races and games. A popular sport was **chariot** (CHAIR-ee-uht) racing. Races were held in stadiums or **coliseums** (kawl-uh-SEE-uhmz). Thousands of people came to watch the races. Two or four horses pulled the fast chariots. Sometimes elephants or camels were used instead of horses. There could be as many as 24 races in a single day.

Gladiator (GLAD-ee-ay-tuhr) games were also very popular. Men fought against animals and each other. Many men fought to their deaths. It was a very violent, terrible sport. Thousands of people watched the

▼ The ruins of the Roman Colosseum still stand today.

Family Fun

The sports stadium in Rome was called Circus Maximus (MAX-uh-muhs). Men and women were allowed to sit together. So, chariot races became family events. Food and drinks were sold, too.

▲ The Circus Maximus was a popular site for chariot racing.

bloody battles. The huge Colosseum (kawl-uh-SEE-uhm) in Rome was the most famous arena for this event.

Performances in theaters were also a popular pastime. Roman plays were based on plays from ancient Greece. Successful actors were popular like movie stars are today.

The Invention of Pantomime

The Romans invented new ways to perform at the theater. One example was pantomime (PAN-tuh-mime). An actor would dance and mime a story to music.

Famous Heroes

Gladiators were the sports stars of the day. Some of them became rich and famous. It seems strange to people today that Romans liked this type of sport. The violence is much worse than any sport today.

Roman ▶ gladiators were very violent.

THE LANGUAGE OF ROME

Most people in early Rome spoke Latin. Different forms of Latin were used. Everyday speech was one form. A more formal Latin was used in literature and official documents.

Romans learned Latin grammar in school. They learned to write in Latin as well. Many students also learned Greek.

Latin is still used today, but not as often. Medical and legal terms are often Latin words. Latin is also used to **classify** and name plants and animals. However, Latin is rarely spoken today.

Modern languages are heavily influenced by Latin. Many English words have Latin roots or word parts. If you look in a dictionary, you will see many Latin roots for words. Words such as civil, legal, and virus are based on Latin roots.

◀ This stone tablet from the Colosseum is engraved in Latin.

▲ This Bible is written in Latin.

Latin Root	English Meaning	English Example
ami	like, love	amiable
cept	take, hold	intercept
dict	tell	dictate
junct	join	junction
mov	move	immovable
ped	foot	centipede
scrib	write	describe
spect	look	spectator
tract	draw, pull	tractor
vid	see	video

The Influence of Latin

Many important texts were written in Latin. These include poems, literature, and plays. These classical works are still read and taught today.

Alphabet Soup

The English alphabet is based on the Latin alphabet. However, there were only 21 letters in the Latin alphabet. The letter *i* was used for both *i* and *j*. The letter *v* was used for *v*, *u*, and *w*. The letters *y* and *z* were added to the English alphabet later.

GODS AND GODDESSES

Romans believed that Juno protected them.

Early Romans worshipped gods of nature. They made many **sacrifices** (SAK-ruh-fice-ez) to keep the gods happy. They believed that this ensured them a good harvest or clear weather. Romans believed that the gods influenced every part of their lives.

There were three very important gods to the Romans. Jupiter, the sky god, was the most important god. Juno, his wife, was the goddess of women. Their daughter, Minerva, was the goddess of wisdom.

Romans composed myths and legends to tell about how they interacted with the gods. Some myths also explained how events happened in the world around them. These stories told about the mysteries in the world. Many of these mysteries were later explained by science.

The Romans worshipped these gods at festivals. They built many temples in their honor. Romans believed that humans could have god-like qualities. And, emperors were often worshipped as gods.

▲ Jupiter

Naming the Moons

Many moons and stars are named after Roman gods. Planet names, such as Jupiter and Mars, are also taken from names of gods.

A Temple for the Gods

The Pantheon (PAN-thee-awn) was built between A.D. 118 and 125. It still stands in Rome today. In fact, it is one of the best-preserved examples of Roman architecture.

◀ The Pantheon was a temple built to honor the gods.

CHRISTIANITY IN ROME

Romans were **tolerant** of other religions. Christianity, however, was an exception. Christians were often attacked for their beliefs. They did not offer sacrifices to Roman gods. This made many Romans angry.

In A.D. 64, a great fire almost destroyed all of Rome. Nero, the emperor, blamed Christians for the fire. He outlawed the religion. Christians had to worship in secret. This went on for 200 years. The Christians were afraid of being **persecuted** (PUHR-sih-kyoot-ed). Many Christians were killed in horrible ways.

▼ Vatican City is located in the middle of Rome.

◀ There are many Catholic churches in Italy.

Later, Emperor Constantine felt differently about Christianity. He made Christianity an official religion in Rome. Rome became a very important city for Christians.

Constantine ▶ was a Christian.

The Vatican

Vatican City is the center of the Roman Catholic Church today. The pope lives and works there. He is the leader of the Catholic Church.

Latin Mass

Catholic services used to be said only in Latin. Then, speaking Latin became very rare. So, the people attending mass did not understand what the priests were saying. The church decided to change its policy. They wanted people to understand mass. Now, Catholic masses are said in whatever language is spoken by the people in the church.

FAMOUS ROMAN EMPERORS

Many men who ruled over the Roman Empire are important historical figures. Augustus is famous for being the first Roman emperor. He worked hard to strengthen the Roman Empire. He cleaned up the city streets. He also built many new buildings. He even organized the city into districts.

Not all emperors were as successful. Caligula (kuh-LIG-yuh-luh) was Rome's third emperor. He became mentally ill. He went mad and was **assassinated** (uh-SAS-suh-nate-ed). Emperor Commodus (KAWM-uh-duhs) also went crazy while in office.

▲ The Washington Monument is named after the first president of the United States.

Trajan was emperor when Rome reached its greatest size. He was a talented military commander. He built Trajan's Forum during his **reign**. This forum included Trajan's column. It still stands in Rome today.

◀ Images of Roman life on a close-up of Trajan's Column

A Monumental Honor

Countries often name monuments after leaders. Trajan was a very important leader in the Roman Empire. So, he has special monuments named after him. In the United States, there are many monuments named for important leaders.

Coins

Some Roman emperors were honored in a special way. Their pictures were placed on Roman coins. Countries still honor important people by placing their images on money.

THE EMPIRE FALLS

The Roman Empire collapsed in A.D. 476. How did such a powerful empire fail? Its large size made it hard to **govern**. This meant it was hard to rule over all the Roman people. Long borders also made it weak and easy to attack. The army could not fight enemies in so many places. So, Rome's enemies continued attacking until they weakened the borders.

THE ROMAN EMPIRE
CIRCA A.D. 395

Provinces

PREFECTURE OF GAUL
DIOCESE OF SPAIN
1. Baetica, 2. Lusitania, 3. Galicia,
4. Tarraconensis, 5. Carthaginiensis,
6. Mauretania Tingitana
7. Balearic Isles.
DIOCESE OF GAUL
1. Viennensis, 2. Lugdunensis,
3.-4. Germania I. II.
5.-6. Belgica I. II.
7. Maritime Alps.
8. Pennine and Graian Alps.
9. Maxima Sequanorum,
10.-11. Aquitaine I. II.
12. Novempopulana,
13.-14. Narbonensis I. II.
DIOCESE OF BRITAIN
1. Maxima Caesariensis, 2. Valentia,
3.-4. Britain I. II.
5. Flavia Caesariensis.

PREFECTURE OF ITALY
DIOCESE OF AFRICA
1. Byzacium, 2. Numidia,
3. Tripolitana,
4. Mauretania Sitifensis
5. Mauretania Caesariensis
DIOCESE OF THE CITY OF ROME
1. Campania, 2. Tuscany and Umbria,
3. Picenum Suburbicarium, 4. Sicily.

5. Apulia and Calabria,
6. Bruttia and Lucania,
7. Samnium, 8. Sardinia,
9. Corsica, 10. Valeria.
DIOCESE OF ITALY
1. Venetia and Istria,
2. Aemilia, 3. Liguria,
4. Flaminia and Picenum Anno-
narium, 5. Cottian Alps,
6.-7. Raetia I. II. 8. Pannonia II.
9. Savia, 10. Pannonia I., 11. Dalmatia,
12. Noricum mediterraneum,
13. Noricum ripense,
14. Valeria ripensis.

PREFECTURE OF ILLYRICUM
DIOCESE OF MACEDONIA
1. Macedonia, 2. Crete, 3. Thessaly,
4. Epirus vetus, 5. Epirus nova,
6. Macedonia Salutaris.
DIOCESE OF DACIA
1. Dacia mediterranea, 2. Moesia I.,
3. Praevalitana, 4. Dardania,
5. Dacia ripensis.

PREFECTURE OF THE EAST
DIOCESE OF EGYPT
1. Upper Libya, 2. Lower Libya,
3. Thebais, 4. Egypt, 5. Arcadia,
6. Augustamnica.

DIOCES
1. Palestine
3. Syria I.
5. Cyprus, 6.
7. Palestine
8. Phoenicia
9. Eufratens
11. Osrhoëne,
13. Cilicia II.,
15. Arabia.
DIOCE
1. Bithynia,
3. Paphlago
5. Galatia, S
6.-7. Cappado
8. Helenopon
9. Pontus Po
10.-11. Armeni
DIOC
1. Pamphylia
3. Caria, 4. I
5. Lycaonia,
7. Phrygia I
8. Phrygia I
DIOCE
1. Europe, 2.
3. Haeminon
4. Rhodope,
6. Scythia.

its of the Roman Empire
indaries of dioceses

t of a metropolitanate (archbishopric)
t of a bishopric
.- DIOCESE, P.- PROCONSULATE

▲ This 1905 image shows a busy bridge in Constantinople

The empire was divided into two halves. The Eastern Empire lasted 1,000 years more than the Western Empire.

However, the importance of ancient Rome lives on today. People around the world are still impacted by the ancient Romans. This keeps the empire very much alive. It proves just how strong the Roman Empire really was.

Rome in Turkey?

The capital of the Eastern Empire was Constantinople (kawn-stan-tuh-NO-puhl). Today, this city is called Istanbul (is-tan-BOOL). It is located in Turkey. Many Roman buildings still stand in Turkey.

The European Union

Today, countries in Europe make up the European Union. These countries cover a lot of the same land as Rome did. But, the European Union is not one nation like the Roman Empire. The leaders of the countries work together. They want unity among the different nations.

GLOSSARY

aqueducts—pipes or channels used to carry water

assassinated—murdered someone by a surprise attack

chariot—two-wheeled, horse-drawn vehicle that was used in races

citizens—members of a state or nation who owe allegiance to its government and are entitled to its protection

classify—to arrange or assign to groups

coliseums—large sports stadiums

dictator—someone who has total control of a country

gladiator—a person who engaged in a fight, often to the death, for public entertainment

govern—to rule or exercise authority over

heir—someone who receives property or titles when another person dies

legionnaires—foot soldiers of the Roman army

persecuted—continually treated in a cruel and harmful way

plebeians—common people of Rome who fought for more rights

reign—the time period that a person rules

republic—a country whose rulers are elected by the people

Roman numerals—a system of numbers based on an ancient Roman system

sacrifices—acts of offering something to the gods

slaves—people who are owned by others and have no personal rights

stylus—an ancient writing instrument, used to write on wax tablets

togas—loose outer garments worn in public by ancient Romans

tolerant—showing an acceptance of others' feelings or beliefs that may be different from one's own

villas—large country homes

INDEX

IMAGE CREDITS